MIDNIGHT MUSINGS

Neelam Rangwala Shah

BookLeaf Publishing
India | USA | UK

Presentation by *BookLeaf Publishing*

Web: www.bookleafpub.com

E-mail: info@bookleafpub.com

ISBN:9789363312067

First edition 2024

DEDICATION

I firstly dedicate this little booklet to caffeine, its indigenous powers to keep my sleep away facilitated me to scribble all that you readers will hopefully rejoice.

Nothing can be possible without my parents who have taught me all I know.

I express gratitude to my family and friends for being around.

Also finally acknowledge the publishers for this opportunity.

ACKNOWLEDGEMENT

A big thank you to Kartik, my partner and companion, who in the process of reading my poems started talking in rhymes – an interesting kind of motivation.

I also want to thank my two dear sisters for believing that I will be able to scribble these poems in a row.

Finally, a huge thanks to my little niece, Jainee for her amazing photographic skills which is the cover page of this little booklet. She has captured the night life of my city in the most dashing manner, I could not have thought of any better cover page.

A STRANGER's SMILE

The door of the lift opens
And I see a smiling face
Her eyes sparkle in tons
Oh! Such outstanding grace!

I've seen her earlier too
Racing up and down
Who is she, I have no clue
A beautiful little girl in town.

Is it mere coincidence
To bump into her once or twice
Her sight gets me smiling at each
instance
In my life, I feel a spice.

How should I talk to her, I have no clue
But I'm eager to see her soon
As her smile drives away my blue
Making me whistle in perfect tune.

A stranger she is, I seldom see
But she feels so familiar
A person I will like to speak to with glee
Hours together moments to blabber.

Some people we know not
But the heart feels a connect
So, I have her in my thought
And I wish her smile is always perfect.

****

SANDWICHED

 I picked up two slices of bread
And wondered what I should spread,
Quickly went on some coriander dip
While I was speculating what I could sip.

Sliced cucumber and tomatoes were
layered
Spices sprinkled, dish mouth smacking
flavored,
Then laid a few patties with vegetables
loaded
Followed by plentiful mozzarella and
cheddar shredded.

Mayonnaise with crunchy leaves resting
Oh! the second slice goes up hopping,
These beautiful layers, crispy and
colorful
Get grilled and become more pleasureful.

A sight that can tempt us all
Its aroma alone will call,
A sandwich is not just layers of food
But also, various thoughts in my head
glued.

Food when hot, crusty and vibrant
Peps up a mood and keeps me pleasant,
Add to this a drink – coffee or tea
With the added caffeine, I will be me.

A sandwich of thoughts makes me anxious
Being squeezed amongst loved ones, I'm
gracious,
This is another sandwich I love to be in
Where on my face, there's always a grin.

But I deal with some other sandwich daily
While sitting in vehicles moving on roads
slowly,
In traffic, multi-colored cars tip-toeing
Due to the delay even I am whining.

Every sandwich has a tale to tell
All wonderfully curated, varied emotions
to spell,
Can I enjoy the traffic with music playing
Dancing while seated instead of
grumbling.

Or churn my thoughts around
When I'm taken away from the ground,
Deep breathe while birds are chirping
Rejoice sunsets with my dreams flapping.

For now, I need to get back to the best
sandwich of all
Delectable in front of me standing tall,
Crispy and gooey, warm and comforting
Enjoying every bite, a feeling so
satisfying.

****

VITAMIN - G

The week can get exhausting
Until arrives a Friday
Come dusk and every sensation is tingling
Hoping it is not a dry day.

All of us have sailed on this boat
Waiting for the working week to conclude
And on this realistic note
Don't pick up the television remote and
get glued.

Let's pull up a back-pack
And throw in a few essentials
Head countryside to live in a shack
Leisure full of potentials.

Waking to the crowing rooster
Dancing to the rhythm of hummingbirds
Even the little blades of grass chatter
Through emotions and not words.

Step on mother earth with ease and calm
Admiring patterns of dews as they plop
Chill beneath your feet has its own charm
Oh! With this alone, the fun doesn't stop.

Every tree has a calling
And the birds sense this fast
Hastily they will be flying
This sight is such a blast.

Leaves around are refreshingly green
The aroma of flowers fills the air
Lush shades can only be seen
Enjoy this solitude – pull up a chair.

The sun has just risen
It's rays glittering gold
Planting a kiss straight from heaven
One we all will always want to hold.

Attempt watering some plants
This too is rejuvenating
Fiddling with the soil can feel like trance
This state of mind is a blessing.

So, lets soak in this VITAMIN – G
Prancing with leaves – small and big
It will fill your heart and keep you jolly
Until your feet dance a jig.

Nature is a cure
To keep our senses intact
A get-away all will love for sure
None needs proof for this fact.

****

SUNSETS

Sunsets by the sea are an experience
With the big bright ball diving
His reflection adds to his radiance
While the water is happily grooving.

The waves play chinese whispers
Exchanging messages between the sun
and the shore
They are loyal secret keepers
They rhythmically swash and not snore.

The sky is luminous
Filled with warm colours endless
Bright and pastels, both, we can witness
Every sunset is pretty and priceless.

Gradually blues and purples takeover
Subtilling the earthy colours
Wish the sun at the horizon could stay
forever
So, the atmosphere permanently glitters.

We see cotton balls up there
So fluffy and comforting
These clouds with golden lining look
solitaire
Rays from behind them emerging.

Sunsets can be fancy
Hues of orange, peach, yellow and red
Epitome of warmth and vibrancy
'God is painting the sky', it's said.

****

MOSQUITO BITE

A mosquito bite
Can be quite a sight
Making pink out of white
While the skin gets puffy slight.

This creature
Being opportunist in nature
Any part of your skin they will capture
Stinging they will paint picture.

It could be your nose
That it choose
Before you oppose
Your blood goes.

So dress with care
And do not bare
Unless you wish to dare
Cuz your blood, it will not spare.

****

PATIENTS DOC

A cough or a sneeze
Or a tummy that isn't at ease,
An ache of every kind
Or when vitamins, blood can't find,
We knock the doors of a medico
His knowledge and experience magnifico.

There is a little old man
Who by mere touch can scan,
He then creates a combination of tablets
Colourful little droplets,
Pop them thrice a day
And you will no longer be grey.

Then comes the sophisticated ones
Requiring tests and scans in tons,
Who end up scribbling prescriptions
Combinations of antibiotics and
injections,
It could give a hole to your pocket
But will get you ready to fly a rocket.

My favourite doctor
Is full of laughter,
This cute looking one
Full of fun,
Drives fear out of the patient
Then talks about the ailment,
Prescribes a few pills
To eradicate the ills,
The patient may walk it weary and
worn-out
But he will step out, half cured wanting to
hangout.

These docs play a pivotal role
Their patient's recovery being their goal,
Best achieve success giving comfort
A sweet smile will never hurt,
Look after the psychology of the ailing
Medicines will then be aiding,
A quick recovery together facilitating
As all ills are gradually curing,
A happy inmate will be dancing
In whose glory the doctor will be basking.
****

INDIAN SUMMER

We wake up to a docile little ball
Cutely winking to us all,
Around six it peeps out
From slumber to a perfect pout,
Waiting for us to sip our cuppa of tea
Until then he is lazily smiling at us, with
glee,
Now as though himself high on caffeine
His true glory is seen.

In this scorching heat
Wish we could stay off the street,
Nest in our office cabins
Indoors hidden behind curtains,
Outdoor is a furnace
Could light up a fire in its harshness,
Sweat trickling down all day
Everyone is irritable and tired all the way

We reach out to a sunscreen
Apply in the morning and in between,

As we can't afford to scream
'Has our skin dyed so supreme?',
Jazzy glares to cover the eyes
Being delicate, need a prize,
A trick to be the cool dude
Before the heat gets us chewed.

Flowy linens are best to wear
Light colours for outwear and sportswear,
One may choose to bare the skin
But don't forget to carry a napkin.
Hats and caps are out of the closet
Let head and neck not be sun's target
Scarves and bandanas tied around
And feet tucked safe in the shoe on the
ground.

Our saviour is water
Sip it all day to feel better,
Jump into the pool if you can
You will hop out with a tan,
Cold packs can help too
We all will look red and feel blue,
But summers can bring us a smile

And give reasons to celebrate in style.

My dearest friend – the air cooler
It too is exhausted, awaiting a breather
It isn't as faithful now,
How I wish it vents out snow somehow.
As the sun blesses us with more heat
Around the bush, we cannot beat,
My brain finds ways to chill,
To beat this heat and not grill.

****

MY CITY'S SKYLINE

I am from the city that never sleeps
Twenty-four by seven, it beeps,
Attracting people from all over
They come with dreams and hangover,
Thus, has grown this city
From seven islands to a place mighty,
And so has changed our skyline
And now also our shoreline.

I was surrounded by the sea
Beaches and waves around me,
Endless water is such a fancy
Shades of blue till eyes can see,
This view has now got tipsy
Due to the infrastructure policy,
Bridges and highways have blocked my vision
The feeling of endlessness is now hidden.

The tallest structure was a chimney
Used by textile mills in their company,

These were two hundred feet tall
To release the smoke far away from all,
Houses were just a couple of level
The horizon being an easy visual,
But now there are skyscrapers
everywhere
Fifty to hundred levels in the air.

Sunsets are going to be best seen online
Visuals captured by the drone shall shine,
Moonrise is going to be a surprise
As I will never see it in the skies,
People may live amongst the clouds
Through their houses a passage allowed,
Development has surely changed the
skyline
Taking nature away from me for which I
whine.

****

FOODIE

I love food
Both eating and cooking
In the kitchen I'm often glued
Whisking up a meal tempting.

India, being a vast country
Houses recipes in plenty
Every delicacy is a chemistry
Proportions and combinations creating
beauty.

Idli is my favourite breakfast
This humble dish also enjoys variations
Masala, thate, rava, buttered, fried – all a
blast
A beautiful beginning for the days
actions.

Dosas are another culinary delight
They can be stuffed or plain
Crispy, thin and savory in every bite

Happiness after this meal, I can't explain.

Dhokla's have travelled around the world
Returning back experienced and wise
Chinese, Mexican, Italian and Sandwiched
they swirled
Giving the khaman importance pennywise.

Our flat breads are a platter on their own
Rumali- the thinnest and Sirman – the
bulkiest
Plain or stuffed; all are known
Bite into them to stay for long fullest.

Curries prepared spicy and hot
Housing vegetables or lentils in them
plenty
Roti or rice together sought
Drizzle ghee before hogging at the party.

How can I forget the quick snack
All kinds of charts – tangy and crunchy
Sev-puri, pani-puri or bhel lay on the rack
All of them mouth-watering and munchy.

Another snack close to my heart
Wada's and bhajiyas of all kinds
Vegetables dipped in chickpea flour is an
art
Longing to bite into them, my teeth
grinds.

Desserts can leave me speechless
From halwas and gulab jamuns warm and
soft
To kheer and rasgullas that gulp down
effortless
And ladoos and barfi's I love a lot.

In every fun, there is food
Salty or sweet is based on mood
And if the tummy is full
Worry not, a drink wont be harmful.

Summarising some of my favourite
delicacies
Has gotten me longing for some
I will reach out for some cottage cheese

Marinated and grilled - a meal wholesome.

****

UP ABOVE THE WORLD SO HIGH

In Mumbai you can barely see a star
With the city lights in full glory at every
hour,
But up above from my residence
I saw airplanes in abundance.

With the city being high on air traffic
Seeing propellers of the planes were
classic,
As they took off from the runway
Right above my house was their pass way.

In the night these planes glittered
Their lights beautifully featured,
While their wheels retract into the wings
A musical hum it sings.

As a child I waved at each plane passing
by
Even though it was really high,
I felt the pilot saw me
Happily smiling until it flee.

During the day I played a guess game
Identifying flights based on time it came,
The logos of each airline were memorised
Correct answers were prized.

I was not from the internet age
My knowledge was reading page by page,
Speaking to engineers for information
few
Why it did not move its wings, I had no
clue.

Looking down, I'd see its shadow run by
And then up quickly to see it fly by,
My entire house its shadow would
consume
A huge monster in the air going zoom.

The further it went, the smaller it got
Its real size, couldn't imagine, just
thought,
Loaded with people and things in plenty
Looking at me through those windows'
dainty.

Birds are light, so they could fly
The plane was huge and heavy but still in
the sky
Like an eagle effortlessly it soared
While I, standing below, wished I was
aboard.

****

BOOKS - BEST INFLUENCERS

I grew up reading Enid Blyton
'Noddy' – a giver, who helps selflessly
With his cute smile, my heart he won.

'Naughtiest Girl Series' – a masterpiece
While things kept going wrong for her
My first lessons in mischief, I learnt in
ease.

My idea of mystery is rooted deep within
Through plots formulated by *Agatha
Cristine*
Suspense and surprise, my head can spin.

Jane Eyre gave me lessons on love
With fondness and emotions treasured,
not looks
Happily, ever after, is great; hold onto
the dove.

'*Little Women*' got family values

To work on flaws, evolve and learn from
them
When things go wrong, snooze, don't
express views.

'*Alice in Wonderland*' was my first take on
horror
But it made me accept change
As I will also be a different person now
than earlier.

'*Sharp wit and pair of fine eyes*' matter
more than dress
Is a learning from '*Pride and Prejudice*'
Passion and reason in love – it express.

'*Harry Potter*' opened up my imagination
To a world of magic where dreams come
true
While expressing a whirlpool of emotion.

'*The Power of Now*' forced me to live in
the present

Letting go of the baggage of yesterday
and fear of tomorrow
Rejoicing every moment as it is brilliant.

Our books are beautiful influencers
Subtly and sweetly injecting life lessons
Which, if instructed by elders, are
blabbers.

Let's inculcate in kids the habit of
reading
Read along at times too
Discuss the books while happily chatting.

Their young minds will soak in values
Instructions and preaching are a passé
Books can then remain their forever
gurus.

****

APRIL ONE

Making others a fool is always fun
Few harmless jokes cracked
But be prepared to run
If the other is too much jacked.

April fool's day I have always looked
forward to
Planning and preparation taking a week
Thus, suspense only brew
Care taken for the idea not to leak.

My favourite targets were grandpa and
granny
Who innocently got trapped every year
From my plot they couldn't flee
Ending in smiles from ear to ear.

Grandpa was scared of insects and
rodents
Which I could strategically place around
Beetroot like rats' tails hid stagnant

Or clay insects stuck to walls were found.

Grandpa would scream and screech
Often get up on the chair
Grab a stick, a creature to reach
To drive it out in thin air.

Granny had friends many
Thus, blank calls worked wonders
A secret lover calling her for tea
Had I been caught; i'd be in the grinder.

My nephew seems to have taken over me
Tricking his mommy to a plate of brownies
Temptation for a dessert got steamy
And arrived a plate with two brown "E's".

Marking of a red lip on a collar
A girl friend it can piss
Try this out on her
But be ready to pacify with many a kiss.

Another trick is a fake plaster

An arm in the sling
Cook up stories without a laughter
Even when it's a fling.

This one day is for harmless tricks
Making noise and screaming too
Pull up your socks for fun and frolics
Scream "Happy Fool's Day to you !!"

****

MAKING A HOME

Purchasing a house can be stressful
As we count our pennies
But seeing it in the making is blissful
Our head and heart say cheese!

Then comes the day
Our feet get to step in
Even bare walls ask us to stay
Our hearts now grin.

Next is furnishing the place nice
For which ideas are bubbling
It surely comes with a price
The place must be functional and
appealing.

Measurements are taken
For things to find its way
Up go the curtain
Ready is our getaway.

The challenge begins here
Making this house a cozy paradise
Full of laughter and cheer
And moments sprinkled with a pinch of
spice.

Vessels in the kitchen will rattle
As we cook meals few
Let our words not battle
And keep us blue.

Our hearts this home symbolizes
Our fondness it should spell
Amongst music and dances
Mainly sweet memories to excel.

Let's raise a toast to our togetherness
And rejoice this strong bond
Lead a life with kindness
Softly and fondly respond.

****

H2O

Pitter patter comes the rain
Little droplets on the window pane
Let's stretch to feel these pearls
Time to rejoice both boys and girls.

The best mornings are seeing dew drops
From one leaf to another it hops
Sparkling shining in the sunrays
Almighty's creations are a praise.

By the sea, the waves gush
Relax in its music – stay hush
It calms every beautiful mind
Nature's reminder to be kind.

From between the mountains
Water paves way in millions
From heights its tumbling down
Despite lots of effort – no frown.

Water in lakes is serene
Crystal clear its seen
In itself its happy
Contented and always chirpy.

Backyards and houses have fountains
Trickling sounds of water lightens
Bringing home a piece of nature
Its tranquility a big feature.

Splashing, kicking and diving
In the pool we love swimming
Feels like lying in a sapphire
In this serenity to retire.

Feeling stressed drink some water
This magical liquid will make you better
Giving energy to wade through
Easing complicated thoughts in queue.

Water is quite underrated you see
Its miraculous qualities are free
Jump and splash around enjoyably
Or happily slurp and sip this beauty.

WHO AM I?

"*Mirror, Mirror on the wall*
Who is the fairest of them all?",
Listening to these, I grew
Expectations from self, I drew.

A clean complexion is a boon
Fairness creams will do the rest soon,
Straight, long hair is beautiful
Else hit the salon, return youthful.

Looks are given undue attention
Tall, thin, fair being accepted notion,
Am I only what sees the eye?
Really, who am I?

A daughter, a sister, a wife, a friend
Various relations penned,
While I am happy to share my pie
Really, who am I?

Grades with A+ and A
Degrees plentiful before me lay,
Through education I touched the sky
Really, who am I?

A chirpy colleague, an easy going boss
Fancy titles beside my name emboss,
Up the corporate ladder wearing a tie
Really, who am I?

A painter, a chef, an artist
My creations on display finest,
My passions give me fame and a high
Really, who am I?

A villa, a car, a beautiful home
Vacations overseas to roam,
Loads of luxuries I can buy
Really, who am I?

It's said, I'm not what I can see
A pretty body smiling with glee,
Hidden in this shape lies a soul
Keeping it pure should be our goal.

It's this soul that's living through me
My good deeds will set it free
With self-actualization and
self-realisation
On a peaceful road to salvation.

Do what's to be done
Enjoy life, have fun,
Live in the present, focus within
Cuz there is more to life than what's in
this skin.

****

FRIDAY ROCKS

A car loaded with friends few
Drove down to wash off our weeks blue,
In the darkness of empty lanes
Vroom, we eradicate our pains,
The street lights were flashing so
A reminder to go with the flow,
And then the clock struck ten
Yuppie!! It's time to feel zen.

A huge bronze gate welcomed us
Heavy, oh what a fuss,
As the doors opened, a chill is felt
Transition from equator to polar belt,
The place is diffusely lit
But our spirit it will kick,
At a distance huge garage lights hung
Romantic radiance sprung,
Pleasing aroma fills the air
Let's rejoice, pull up the chair.

The music is electrifying
It will get your mood flying,
The twang of the guitarist
His strings playing rightist,
The roll of the drums
Results in tapping feet, moving bums,
The casio rings a happy tune
Its energetic rhythm is a boon,
The saxophone dazzles various beats
Eventually, it will get us off our seats.

Music, like an ocean, sweeps me away
To a fantastic zone, full of play,
Loud beats cause thunder in my head
Soft ones make me want to go to bed,
The music in here was just what we
needed
With live singing, playlist curated,
Peppy bollywood songs of 90's sung
Our souls touched, felt young,
He had a soothing voice
Together all of us rejoice.

Take my hand, let's dance
Together feel the trance,
With my husband, in his arms
Rekindling our bond and its charms,
My heart skipped a beat
When he lifted me off my feet,
Holding his finger, I twirled
Roundabout, in my little world,
As the song concluded
A passionate kiss yielded.

Out with friends is a different ballgame
We don't need to behave within the
frame,
Dance to hearts content
Or chill to any extent,
Raising a toast to our friendship
Chilled mocktails we sip,
Fridays can never get better
Amongst company we happily chatter.

****

FRIENDS

I grew in a little society
With company in plenty,

We were about forty
Girls and boys being naughty,

Friendship was about playing together
Fun and frolic with lots of laughter,

Competitions – cycling and art
And chit-chats from the heart,

As I grew, associations swelled
With both girls and boys, I gelled,

In college, hormones of most began
talking
With romantic engagements people
clinging,

I still valued the friendships above all
And stayed away from cupid's call,

Education was priority and I am glad
I didn't get carried away by the fad,

My best buddies were generally boys
Conversations with them, always joys,

We constantly had words to exchange
Topics could often be strange,

Gradually proposals came up my way
But couldn't sway my feet away,

"No thanks, but let's be friends,
With these strings, fun ends,"

My reply was always so simple
With a smile, flaunting my dimple,

Relationship with opposite sex can be
optima
Full of purity, sans drama,

Conversations plenty we can rejoice
Engrossed in each other's voice,

Keeping cupid far away
He with 'Psyche' rejoicing in play,

Girls & boys can't be friends, is believed
Innocence of the heart be perceived,

Our books and media often sow the seed
Of romantic love that creeps in full
speed,

Fondness is the key between any two
Else we will be strangers in a zoo,

Let's be accepting and welcoming
Giving young minds space for blooming,

Rejoicing conversations with the opposite
sex
Keeping it simple and surely not complex,

Comfort swells between two souls
Let's also enjoy it with no trolls.

****

NUMBERS

As a tiny tot
Lessons in numbers I got,
"Ten tiny fingers, ten tiny toes
Two round eyes and one little round
nose",
Mummy sang this to me always
Her simile face I would gaze,
While she got me ready for the day
These numbers my attention would sway,

Older I got
Me, these digits caught,
Monkeys jumped on the bed
And broke their head,
To teach me number
In a manner for me to remember,
Gradually they got my head cracking
Adding, subtracting, multiplying and
dividing,
Loads of formulae hopped around
Only on paper everything was sound,

Until it took me to a complicated pathway
Geometry was fun – a happy get away,
Algebra's 'x's' and 'y's' forced me to ponder
Why did I need the value, I wonder,
Trigonometry took my straight to hell
These calculations made me yell.

Numbers have their own story
A history with its own glory,
India is the hero
Introducing to the world, zero,
The Arabs coined one to nine
Initiating the counting system fine,
These then developed a funny tune
For distinguishing them – a boon,
Lucky number remains seven
While *two little legs* is eleven,
Thirteen is the *unlucky one*
Seventy-one is *bang on the drum*,
Eighty -one became *fat lady with a stick*
Eighty-six was coined *between the sticks*,
Bingo gave numbers a twist
Hilarious descriptions in the list.

Paint by number is how it all began
For identifying them correctly, a plan,
Math-a-magic got me interested in
calculations
Creating different permutations and
combinations,
As a family we enjoyed monopoly
Value of money learnt modestly,
Sudoku is now a craze
Placing numbers in a maze,
Technology elevated zeros and ones
These binary digits play the drums,
Online games are now the in thing
A click and it will spring,
2048 helps destress
Numbers doubling with keys press,
Abacus made calculations faster
The kids are a master.

While studying, the only numbers that
mattered
Were those affecting grades and keeping
us flattered,

Now these precious numbers hold a rank
Only if in maximum they park in the bank,
The deadly ones are what the optician
gives
Smaller ones is what we hope to live,
Numbers also run like horses
Ticking in the clock with full forces.

****

ZZZZZZzzzzz

A little angel picked up a bucket
Filled loads of black paint in it,
On the cloud, this kid sat leisurely
Poured it on earth with glee,
Thus, when I looked out of the window
Pitch dark was the meadow,
This angel was very naughty
But with a hallow roaming chirpy,
Making night out of day
And forcing me to stop play.

My childhood imaginations
Came with weird notions,
I wished the angels mum was mine
So being mischievous would be fine,
The hallow would overpower my horns
All fun, no warns,
No time to waste in bed
Stay up and play instead,
Rolly-Polly with mum would suffice
For my energy levels to spice.

But studying took over playtime
With book in hand, closed eyes were mine,
I could snooze both day and night
It didn't matter whether dark or bright,
Hard books as pillows also felt like cotton
Off the chair, umpteen times I've fallen,
Alphabets and numbers dancing in my dreams
Sometimes they would also eat ice-cream,
Even though the pressure to study creep
I would be fast asleep.

I have a unique relation with slumber
In the night I'm as energetic as flubber,
As the clock strikes twelve
Ideals in my head dwell,
I'm transformed into an owl
Diligently functioning, no fowl,
My eyes shut wee hours of the morn
And from the world I'm torn,
In my blanket wrapped like a frankie
Pillows around, hugging a monkey.

Snoring loud like a pig's snort
While thoughts in my head sort,
During which I can also babble
Entertaining all with a silly fable,
I may answer world toughest questions
too
But on waking up would have no clue,
Twisting and turning all along
In dreamland, singing a song,
Merrily dancing I may hop on a flight
And on this note, wish all a Good Night!!

****

COOLERS

In this scorching heat
I cannot laze and sleep away,
Best to find a treat
To keep cool all day.

Coffee flavoured ice
In chilled milk pops,
A sweetener adds the spice
A divine beverage crops.

Iced tea has variations plenty
These flavours are refreshing,
Grab this chilled drink and flee
With boba's in your mouth popping.

For the fruit friendly
Mocktails and milkshakes are around,
Every combination is a beauty
In the taste, happily drowned.

I pull out a popsicle
So colourful they look,
Daily suck into a couple
While snuggling with a book.

I can scream for ice-cream
Soft, smooth and freezing,
Share it with my team
This companionship is pleasing.

I welcome the king of fruits
Biting into mangoes is divine,
My happiness it boosts
Every invitation it can outshine.

The lazy prefer 'aam ras'
It forms a main course and a dessert,
Bowls go down the throat with no fuss,
With chocolate, this combo can flirt..

Its raw version is equally a delight
Relax, sipping a drink of raw mango
For this weather, it's a match right,
'Aam panha' is cooling so.

Every corner will have a lemonade stall
Or some buttermilk for all,
Kokam juice can make body temperature
fall
These coolers will keep me standing tall.

Sip and run, instead of crawl
As the heat can make us skip a beat
Better to stay hydrated than fall,
As these drinks will keep us sweet and
neat.

Flavoured sodas are an option
From the rack, pick in ease,
Let's for now smile under the sun
Awaiting the monsoon breeze.

****

BOOZE IN THE AIR

Grades not as per expectation
Dreams not in motion,
Elders' advices overpowering
Relation with special friend warring,
Career not taking the required path
Income and expense not doing the math.

A clash between head and heart
Or the heart struck with a dart,
Bad days come anytime
And that is not a crime,
Life makes you the Greek god – Atlas
And everything seems fruitless.

Being a *dude* amongst friends
As with them time spends,
A social life prestigious
In their presence life is joyous,
Could be reasons to pick up the glass
Cheers is being high class.

Boys favourite is chilled beer
Few cans down get them in gear,
Girls prefer a cocktail with vodka
It could be a spicy mix with paprika,
These are easy modes of jiving
Amongst friends in the disc weaving.

Breezer comes in adorable flavours
The sweet tooth it pampers,
Gin and tonic are a summer drink
In these flavours one can sink,
Gobble them to swing
No thoughts in head will ring.

Rum can go well with coke
With fruit juices too its flavours evoke,
Whisky is a man's drink
Munch peanuts, let it sync,
This high is to get one dizzy
Couple of pegs to get on drowsy.

Coffee liquor is for the elite
In style, a selfie to tweet,
To celebrate, champagne is popped

A party's climax topped,
Cheers to new beginnings
And accomplished innings.

When sick, sip brandy
Says a Dutch birdie,
Wine – red, white or rose
Calm feelings arose,
A quick solution to relax
By the beach in shacks.

Shots of tequila followed by lime
Has been a classic favourite for a long
time,
Long Island Iced Tea, sip till you drop
Its flavours will make you hop,
Bite into cheese with these
To recover the hangover with ease.

Want some more fun
This too can be done,
Vaping is the present fad
Nicotine will forever have you glad,
Cigarettes are a passé

But your wallet is to have a say.

Hukka bars are floating around
Inhaling flavoured ones drowned
Chewing tobacco is a local relish
Another option if you wish,
This can keep head busy
But beware, it can get you sneezy.

But these really don't address the stress
Nor does it make reap a success,
It only adds to expenses
Consuming you in its clutches,
It could make you sell your home
With wife and children gone.

It could distance from family
And add to misery,
Medically screw you up
Further complications to buildup,
Rising hospital bills
And putting you on pills.

Friends may wave goodbye

Socially there will be no standby,
Studies and career ruined
An entire future darkened,
If looks matter to you
This could keep you blue.

Instead, let's say cheers over water
Enjoy company with blabber,
Step out in nature
Relax while painting a picture,
Light up candles in the house
In its aroma cuddle your spouse.

Let's listen to calming music
Swaying to it can give a kick,
Play with some cute animals
They are full of cuddles,
Spend time with family
Nothing else can keep you happy & bubbly.

****